How to Understand Your Kid Through Effective Parenting

I0558366

A New Way of Being a Parent: Practical Advice for Today's Families from The Heart of Parenting Your Kids

Adegboye S. Aduragbemi

INTRODUCTION

Being a parent is an experience unlike any other; it's full of wonders, difficulties, and happy moments. Managing the duties and complications of parenting in the complicated web of marriage could peradventure prompt concerns about intimacy maintenance, communication, and discipline. For couples about to embark on the life-changing journey of parenthood, this book is a lighthouse of knowledge, providing clarity, insight, and valuable advice to help them manage the challenges with grace and purpose.

In this book, you will find a thorough compilation of frequently asked questions, thoughtful responses, and professional guidance specific to the intricacies of parenting in a married relationship. Every query is answered with compassion, comprehension, and practical advice to help couples successfully navigate the rewards and difficulties of parenthood together, from the delights of bringing a new life into the world to the unavoidable hardships and tribulations of raising children. "How to Understand Your Kid Through Effective Parenting" provides couples with a road map for maintaining a united front, protecting a strong family link, and putting their relationship first despite the demands of motherhood through relevant tales, real-life events, and evidence-based techniques. This book offers priceless ideas and valuable strategies to help you parent with confidence, resiliency, and love—whether you're a first-time parent or navigating the adolescent years.

May you find comfort in other people's experiences that you have shared, inspiration in the knowledge of professionals, and the bravery to accept parenthood as a means of achieving more fulfilment and connection in your marriage as you set out on this path of research and discovery.

Together, let's travel through the ageless issues, complex nuances, and exquisite aspects of married parenthood.

Chapter One

Learning from other's experience

How competing parenting philosophies may strain relationships

Once upon a time, Sarah and Mark were the picture of a contented family living in Sunset Hills. They had a desire to create a family together when they first met in college and fell madly in love. But as they started the adventure of parenthood, competing parenting philosophies and objectives caused their relationship to fall apart.

Sarah was a loving stay-at-home mother who valued emotional bonding with her kids as well as mild discipline. She cherished the time they spent together raising their children and making sure they were in a safe, caring environment. Mark, a prosperous businessman who had high hopes for their kids' development, preferred a more controlled parenting style that placed a strong emphasis on academic performance and discipline.

Although Sarah and Mark's different parenting philosophies initially appeared to be a minor annoyance, tensions increased as their kids became older. Unable to come to an agreement or compromise, they quarrelled nonstop about extracurricular activities, screen time limits, and discipline. Their once-loving relationship turned into a never-ending loop of discontent, hatred, and finger-pointing.

One fateful evening, a heated debate over their son's behaviour turned into a full-blown showdown, bringing their parenting troubles to a peak. Feeling overpowered and abandoned by Mark's dictatorial style, Sarah lost her cool and became enraged, accusing him of being overly strict and demanding with their kids. Frustrated by what he saw as Sarah's lack of consistency and discipline, Mark reacted defensively, refusing to negotiate or even try to reach a solution.

As the years went by, there was no longer any sign of love or connection between Sarah and Mark as their relationship continued to worsen due to their arguments. In a frantic bid to save their marriage, they attempted parenting classes, couples therapy, and even a trial separation, but it didn't work. Ultimately, they both lamented the loss of the family they had previously imagined and made the painful decision to split ways.

Years later, Sarah and Mark coincidentally crossed paths once more. They couldn't help but feel a twinge of grief for the love they had lost as they made small talk. They came to the realization that their failure to work things out as parents had ruined their relationship, and they wished they had placed more emphasis on mutual respect, communication, and compromise early on.

This story above shows how competing parenting philosophies and agendas may strain even the most solid relationships, emphasizing the value of open communication, willingness to make concessions, and support from one another in building strong, long-lasting bonds.

Enduring partnership through love, support, and mutual respect

Sarah and David were two people whose lives in the bustling metropolis of Metroville unexpectedly came together to form a partnership based on love, shared values, and a solid dedication to family. David, a loving father overcoming the difficulties of being a single parent, and Sarah, a committed mother of two with a heart full of love, met at a local parenting support group where they sought advice and encouragement from one another.

Their early exchanges were characterized by empathy and understanding as they grew closer over their experiences and difficulties with childrearing. Whereas David was motivated by Sarah's nurturing personality and her capacity to provide a caring and encouraging atmosphere for her family, Sarah appreciated David's commitment to his children and his steadfast love for them.

Sarah and David found a strong bond and mutual respect as they spent more time together, which developed into a long-lasting partnership. They created a foundation of trust and understanding in their relationship by sharing their hopes, dreams, and worries.

As they handled the pleasures and challenges of raising children together, their shared dedication to parenthood served as the foundation of their relationship. Knowing they were stronger together than apart, Sarah and David accepted their roles as parents and helped each other through milestones, restless nights, and tantrums.

As they relied on one another for support and found happiness and contentment in their joint parenting adventure, their love grew. For their children, Sarah and David established a warm and caring environment full of possibilities, love, and fun.

Amid the presence of their loved ones, including their children, Sarah and David exchanged vows in a moving ceremony as their love grew. They accepted their duties as co-parenting partners, confident that their unwavering passion and commitment to their family would help them overcome any obstacles.

Years later, Sarah and David proudly and gratefully reflected on their experience. They were thankful for the happiness and fulfilment they had found in each other. They understood that their relationship had been based on a solid foundation of love, shared values, and a strong dedication to family. Their relationship had only gotten closer over time, and they were confident that their family would prosper for many generations to come as long as they had each other and their kids as their role models.

This story highlights the value of love, support, and respect for one another in creating a solid and enduring partnership by showing how a relationship can be based on shared motherhood.

Chapter Two

Basis of parenting

How can we work through differences in our marriage's parenting approaches or styles?

It takes mutual respect, honest communication, and a willingness to make concessions to get along when navigating different parenting philosophies. Start by talking about each other's parenting philosophies, values, and preferences. Try to figure out why each person chose the course of action that they did. Find parenting goals and areas of agreement, then collaborate to develop a parenting plan that incorporates elements of both partners' parenting philosophies.

How can we stay a strong and happy couple and still successfully co-parent and share responsibilities?

Clear communication, joint decision-making, and a dedication to supporting one another as parents and partners are all necessary for effective co-parenting. Establish a shared calendar or schedule to manage tasks and activities, and make it a priority to check in on a regular basis to talk about parenting-related issues. In spite of the demands of parenting, schedule regular date nights or quality time as a couple to strengthen your bond and nurture your relationship.

How do we resolve disputes or stress that come with being a parent?

Good communication, empathy, and patience are necessary when managing conflicts arising from parenting stress or disputes. Spend some time listening to one another's worries without passing judgment and being honest about your own emotions. Instead of pointing fingers, let's work together to find solutions. Prioritize supporting one another during difficult times and think about scheduling specific times to have calm, productive conversations about parenting-related issues.

Chapter Three

Striking parental balance in the family

How can we make sure that the way we parent is in line with our goals and values as a couple?

Consciously communicating, reflecting, and working together are necessary to guarantee that parenting methods are in line with shared values. As parents, spend some time discussing and defining your basic principles and beliefs. Together, decide on your family's priorities and common goals. When setting boundaries and making parenting decisions, refer to these values and objectives as a guide. Then, periodically review and tweak your strategy as necessary to keep it in line with your family's shared vision.

How can we strike a healthy balance between our roles as parents and our relationship as a couple while still making self-care a priority?

Making self-care a priority and preserving a harmonious equilibrium between your relationship and parenting calls for

14

deliberate work and dialogue. Schedule regular self-care activities that support your mental, emotional, and physical health, and help one another in doing the same. Plan regular date nights or quality time as a couple. To balance the responsibilities of parenting with the upkeep of a solid and satisfying relationship, place a high value on open communication and mutual support.

How can we, as parents, continue to forge a solid bond and cooperative relationship with one another?

Setting aside quality time as a couple is essential to keeping a strong bond and partnership while raising children. Aside from your parental duties, schedule regular date nights or alone time to strengthen your relationship. Communicate openly about your needs and feelings, and find ways to support each other emotionally and physically. Never forget to thank and appreciate one another for your efforts as parents and in your relationship.

How do we ensure that our parenting responsibilities are balanced with other aspects of our lives, such as work and self-care?

Establishing boundaries and priorities is necessary to maintain a healthy balance between work, parenting, and self-care. Establish a family schedule that includes time set out for personal, professional, and parenting responsibilities. Talk to your partner about your needs and obligations, and work together to find a balance that will benefit you both as a couple and your kids as a whole.

How can we foster a positive co-parenting relationship with our ex-partner if we are divorced or separated?

Fostering a positive co-parenting relationship with your ex-partner requires focusing on the well-being of your children and maintaining open, respectful communication. Keep discussions focused on parenting issues and avoid bringing up past conflicts. Be flexible and willing to compromise when making decisions about your children's upbringing. Seek support from mediators or counsellors if needed to navigate co-parenting challenges effectively.

How can we honour each other's unique parenting roles and contributions while still preserving a strong sense of unity and cohesion as a family?

Promoting open communication, mutual respect, and a shared commitment to supporting each other's parenting roles and contributions are essential to keeping a family cohesive and cohesive. Make sure that everyone feels heard and appreciated by checking in with one another on a regular basis to talk about parenting-related issues. As parents, acknowledge each other's successes and strengths and place a high value on fostering a caring and encouraging environment where everyone feels valued and included.

What tools or networks are available to assist us in overcoming the difficulties and rewards of raising a family while still maintaining a marriage?

Parenting classes, support groups, books, and internet forums are just a few of the tools and networks available to assist couples in navigating the pleasures and difficulties of parenthood. Look for resources that align with your interests and values as a couple, and don't be afraid to ask for help or advice when you need it. Keep in mind that being a parent is a journey, and it's acceptable to ask for assistance and support when needed.

How do we deal with partners' divergent parenting philosophies?

It takes mutual respect, honest communication, and a willingness to make concessions to get along when navigating different parenting philosophies. Start by talking about one another's parenting philosophies and finding points of agreement. Concentrate on the shared values and aspirations you both have for your kids and collaborate to develop a cohesive strategy that respects each partner's viewpoints.

How do we ensure that our parenting responsibilities are balanced with other aspects of our lives, such as work and self-care?

Establishing boundaries and priorities is necessary to maintain a healthy balance between work, parenting, and self-care. Establish a family schedule that includes time set out for personal, professional, and parenting responsibilities. Talk to your partner about your needs and obligations, and work together to find a balance that will benefit you both as a couple and your kids as a whole.

How can we foster a positive co-parenting relationship with our ex-partner if we are divorced or separated?

Fostering a positive co-parenting relationship with your ex-partner requires focusing on the well-being of your children and maintaining open, respectful communication. Keep discussions focused on parenting issues and avoid bringing up past conflicts. Be flexible and willing to compromise when making decisions about your children's upbringing. Seek support from mediators or counsellors if needed to navigate co-parenting challenges effectively.

How can we successfully divide parenting tasks to guarantee fairness and balance between partners?

Dividing parenting chores requires open conversation, recognizing each other's talents and preferences, and creating a division of work that seems equal to both parties. Start by examining each partner's strengths, availability, and preferences when it comes to different elements of parenting, such as childcare, discipline, and household tasks. Consider drafting a shared parenting plan or timetable that explains each partner's responsibilities and allows for flexibility as needed.

What tactics can we employ to manage the stress and overwhelm that often accompany parenting responsibilities?

Managing parenting-related stress and overwhelm needs self-awareness, self-care, and support from your partner. Take pauses when needed and emphasize activities that help you recharge, such as exercise, meditation, or spending time outdoors. Communicate frankly with your partner about your thoughts and wants, and offer each other emotional support and encouragement. Consider obtaining additional help from family, friends, or professional services if needed.

How can we ensure that our parenting decisions are aligned with our shared values and goals as a couple?

Ensuring that parenting decisions correspond with your shared beliefs and goals demands regular discussion, collaboration, and compromise. Take the time to explore your values and interests as parents and establish common ground on crucial subjects such as discipline, education, and family traditions. Keep the lines of communication open as you make decisions

21

together, and be willing to examine and adapt your approach as your children grow and evolve.

How can we retain a strong sense of connection and intimacy with each other while balancing the obligations of parenthood?

Maintaining connection and intimacy in the middle of motherhood demands intentionality and effort from both parties. Make time for regular check-ins and meaningful interactions with your partner, even if it's just a few minutes each day. Prioritize quality time together as a pair, whether it's through date nights, shared hobbies, or small acts of affection. Communicate frankly about your needs and desires, and support each other in finding the balance between your roles as parents and lovers.

What are some successful ways of handling parental guilt and self-doubt?

Managing parental guilt and self-doubt entails practising self-compassion, receiving support from your partner and others, and focusing on the good elements of your parenting efforts. Remind yourself that all parents make errors and that it's appropriate to ask for help when required. Prioritize self-care, find ways to recharge and refresh, and remember that your love and efforts are valuable and appreciated by your children.

Chapter Four

Parent-Children relationship: Bringing the best out of your kid

How can we assist each other as parents while simultaneously prioritizing our unique aims and desires outside of parenting?

Supporting each other as parents while pursuing separate goals involves balance, communication, and teamwork. Take turns helping each other in pursuing your personal interests, hobbies, or job aspirations while also creating time for shared parenting responsibilities and quality time as a pair. Be flexible and willing to adapt your schedules as needed to fit each other's requirements, and prioritize open communication and mutual support in attaining your individual and shared goals.

How do we encourage appropriate boundaries between ourselves and our children while simultaneously fostering a deep and loving relationship?

Encouraging good boundaries with your children entails setting clear expectations, modelling polite behaviour, and offering

24

guidance and assistance as required. Communicate clearly with your children about boundaries and expectations, and be persistent in enforcing rules and punishments. Balance firmness with warmth and compassion, and prioritize spending quality time together to grow your relationship and create trust and mutual respect over time.

What are some practical ways to control sibling rivalry and develop positive sibling relationships within our family?

Managing sibling rivalry entails developing cooperation, communication, and conflict-resolution skills among your children. Encourage empathy and understanding between siblings, and model polite behaviour in your relationships with each other. Create opportunities for your children to bond and participate in everyday activities, and teach them techniques for resolving problems quietly and respectfully. Celebrate each child's abilities and accomplishments, and prioritize developing a caring and loving home environment where everyone feels valued and respected.

How do we handle the obstacles of parenting through different developmental phases, from infancy to adolescence, while keeping a solid and supportive partnership?

Navigating the obstacles of parenting through different developmental phases needs adaptability, patience, and teamwork. Stay knowledgeable about each stage of your child's development and change your parenting technique accordingly. Communicate frankly with your partner about your children's developing needs and habits, and cooperate on solutions for tackling difficulties and supporting their growth and independence. Lean on each other for support and encouragement amid the ups and downs of parenting, and emphasize developing your partnership as the cornerstone for a happy and healthy family life.

How can we handle arguments regarding parenting decisions in front of our children healthily and helpfully?

Navigating arguments about parenting decisions in front of your children needs diplomacy, respect, and a dedication to presenting a united front. If disputes emerge, consider discussing them discreetly and giving a unified decision to your children. Avoid arguing or criticizing each other in front of kids, and prioritize modelling healthy conflict resolution and teamwork.

How can we address conflicts with our children concerning their choices or behaviours courteously and helpfully?

Handling conflicts with your children about their choices or behaviours involves empathy, active listening, and clear communication. Start by recognizing their thoughts and viewpoints before sharing your concerns or demands. Avoid criticizing or ridiculing them, and instead, focus on finding common ground and solutions together. Offer direction and support as needed, and foster open communication and problem-solving abilities.

How can we establish a balance between developing independence in our children and providing direction and support as parents?

Creating a balance between developing freedom and providing guidance entails setting clear expectations, offering chances for growth and learning, and being present to support your children when needed. Encourage your children to take on age-appropriate duties and make decisions independently while still being available to offer direction, support, and reassurance along the way. Allow children to learn from their mistakes, appreciate their accomplishments, and prioritize building their confidence and self-reliance.

How can we handle arguments between our children fairly and impartially?

Handling disagreements amongst your children entails remaining impartial, listening to each child's perspective, and promoting constructive communication and problem-solving abilities. Encourage empathy and understanding among siblings and help them identify and express their feelings healthily. Teach them skills for resolving problems quietly and politely, and offer direction and support as required to reach a conclusion that seems fair and mutually beneficial.

What are some successful ways to promote resilience and coping abilities in our children in the face of adversity or challenges?

Fostering resilience and coping abilities in your children entails providing a caring and nurturing environment, modelling suitable coping mechanisms, and offering chances for development and learning. Please encourage your children to communicate their thoughts and acknowledge their experiences while also helping them develop problem-solving skills and a sense of optimism and self-efficacy. Teach them to adapt to change, bounce back from setbacks, find strength in adversity, and prioritize growing their confidence and resilience over time.

How do we promote our children's hobbies and passions while simultaneously developing a feeling of collaboration and cooperation within our family?

Supporting your children's distinct interests and passions means praising their unique skills and talents, and giving opportunity for them to explore and follow their passions. Encourage open communication and collaboration between siblings and help them discover ways to support and appreciate each other's accomplishments. Foster a spirit of teamwork and cooperation by highlighting the value of working together towards common goals and enjoying each other's triumphs as a family.

How do we handle arguments or disagreements with our children's teachers, caregivers, or other authority figures?

Handling confrontations with authority figures involves diplomacy, persuasion, and a focus on your children's best interests. Approach differences calmly and respectfully, and constructively share your concerns or viewpoints. Seek common ground and ideas that promote your children's well-being and academic achievement. Remember to model polite dispute resolution for your children and teach them how to advocate for themselves positively and assertively.

What tactics can we employ to cultivate a sense of thankfulness and empathy in our children, and why are these qualities crucial for their development?

Raising children with a spirit of appreciation and empathy requires you to set an example of these virtues, provide them with chances to exercise compassion and generosity, and teach them to value the opinions and experiences of others. Encourage your kids to acknowledge the efforts of others and to express thanks for the gifts in their lives. Encourage children to think about the needs and feelings of others and provide them chances to volunteer or participate in service-oriented activities to aid in their development of empathy. These attributes are critical to their growth because they foster wholesome social interactions, mental health, and a feeling of acceptance and connection in their communities.

How can we resolve disputes between our kids in a fair and unbiased way?

Remaining impartial, hearing each child out, and encouraging positive dialogue and problem-solving techniques are all necessary when managing disputes among your kids. Foster compassion and understanding among siblings and assist them in recognizing and expressing their emotions healthily. Instruct them on how to settle disputes amicably and politely and provide assistance when required to arrive at a decision that seems just and advantageous to both parties.

How can we help our kids acquire a feeling of appreciation and empathy, and why are these traits crucial to their growth?

Raising children with a spirit of appreciation and empathy requires you to set an example of these virtues, provide them with chances to exercise compassion and generosity, and teach them to value the opinions and experiences of others. Encourage your kids to acknowledge the efforts of others and to express thanks for the gifts in their lives. Encourage children to think about the needs and feelings of others and provide them chances to volunteer or participate in service-oriented activities to aid in their development of empathy. These attributes are critical to their growth because they foster wholesome social interactions, mental health, and a feeling of acceptance and connection in their communities.

How can we support our kids in acquiring the resiliency and coping mechanisms they need to overcome obstacles and failures in life?

Fostering resilience in your kids entails teaching them healthy coping mechanisms, demonstrating resilience yourself, and creating a safe and nurturing atmosphere for them. Please give them the tools to recognize and communicate their emotions healthily and provide them with the chance to address problems and grow from their errors. Remind them of their skills and capabilities and offer words of support and encouragement. Instruct them on how to deal with change, overcome obstacles, and discover meaning and purpose in trying circumstances.

You can give your kids the fortitude and courage to face life's obstacles by encouraging resilience in them.

What are some strategies for fostering our kids' social and emotional growth, and why is it crucial for their general well-being?

Providing your kids with an opportunity to form healthy relationships, learn how to control their emotions, and grow in empathy and self-awareness is a critical component of supporting their social and emotional development. Help them handle social interactions and problems by supporting them and encouraging them to talk honestly and openly with others. Please enable them to feel accepted and a part of their family and community while also assisting them in acquiring the abilities necessary to succeed in a variety of settings. The development of their social and emotional skills is crucial for their general well-being because it helps them build strong bonds with others, manage stress and hardship, and face obstacles head-on with confidence and resilience.

How can we teach our kids moral principles like kindness, integrity, and respect, and why is it crucial for their character development?

Teaching your kids values like compassion, integrity, and respect entails modelling these traits for them, giving them chances to practice them, and supporting and encouraging them along the way. Help them comprehend the significance of honesty and integrity in their relationships and interactions, as well as the need to treat others with kindness and empathy. Urge children to treat others with respect as well as oneself, and when they do, acknowledge and reward them. These principles serve as the cornerstone of their moral compass, directing their actions and choices for the rest of their lives, which makes them crucial for their character development.

How do we respond when our kids show an interest in pursuits or pastimes that we might not entirely comprehend or endorse?

It takes openness, curiosity, and a willingness to learn to deal with circumstances where your children show interest in pastimes or activities that you may not entirely understand or support. Spend time getting to know your kids' viewpoints and areas of interest by asking them questions that will help you learn more about their drives and passions. Even if their hobbies diverge from your own, keep an open mind and offer encouragement as they explore and come to terms with who they are. Please encourage them to follow their interests and hobbies and provide them with chances to study and develop in fields that enthral and excite them.

What are some ways to help our kids acquire a sense of accountability and responsibility? Why are these traits crucial to their growth?

The best way to help your kids develop a feeling of accountability and responsibility is to give them age-appropriate activities and duties to undertake, as well as to guide and assist them along the way. Motivate children to assist with domestic duties and responsibilities and acknowledge their endeavours and achievements. Help them comprehend the repercussions of their conduct and instil in them the value of keeping promises and carrying out obligations. These attributes are critical to their growth because they foster self-reliance, self-assurance, and a feeling of agency in their life, setting them up for success as adults.

How can we help our kids form wholesome routines and habits like eating right, getting enough sleep, and maintaining an active lifestyle?

Fostering healthy routines and habits in your kids entails setting an example of good conduct, offering direction and encouragement, and fostering an atmosphere that is conducive to wellness. Eat a healthy diet, make exercise a priority, and maintain proper sleep hygiene to set an excellent example for others. Plan and prepare meals with your kids, and encourage them to engage in enjoyable physical activities. To guarantee they receive adequate restorative sleep, establish regular bedtime routines, and restrict screen time before bed. You can assist your children in forming lifelong habits that support their physical, emotional, and mental well-being by making health and well-being a priority as a family.

How can we help our kids succeed academically and be motivated to learn, even in trying circumstances like distance learning or academic failures?

Fostering a happy and encouraging learning atmosphere at home, providing tools and support, and providing direction and help when required are all important ways to boost your children's academic achievement and drive. Establish reasonable expectations and objectives for your kids, and acknowledge and acknowledge their advancements along the road. To ensure kids are focused and organized, set up a unique study space and schedule. You should also give them access to learning resources and materials that are tailored to their interests and learning preferences. Provide affirmation and support to enhance their self-esteem and drive, and remain accessible to assist them in resolving issues and surmounting potential roadblocks during their academic pursuits.

How can we support our kids in learning efficient time management and organizing techniques so they can successfully juggle their academic obligations with extracurricular interests and activities?

You can help your kids acquire good time management and organizing skills by setting an example for them, modelling these behaviours yourself, and providing support and direction as they go. To help them manage their time well, set up a regular daily schedule and habits. You can also help them keep organized by giving them tools and resources like calendars, checklists, and planners. Teach them how to create reasonable goals and deadlines, divide more complex projects into smaller, more manageable segments, and prioritize their workload. As they show growth and improvement, give them credit and encouragement and be there to help and mentor them when needed.

What are some ways that we may assist our kids in developing healthy social skills and forming bonds with their peers, mainly when they might be dealing with issues like bullying or social exclusion?

Promoting communication abilities, empathy, and resilience in your kids is essential. It would be best if you also offered them assistance and direction as they negotiate relationships and social situations. Promote candid dialogue and attentive listening, and assist them in growing in empathy and comprehension of the thoughts and emotions of others. Teach them aggressive and peaceful dispute-resolution techniques and provide them with advice on how to defend others and oneself under challenging circumstances like bullying or social exclusion. Through organizations, community events, and group activities, provide them the chance to form strong relationships with their peers. Additionally, give them encouragement and support when they show kindness, compassion, and friendliness to others.

In the face of obstacles or failures in the classroom, how can we support our kids in cultivating a growth attitude and resilience?

Promoting a positive attitude toward learning and progress, as well as offering support and encouragement when they overcome obstacles and disappointments, are vital components of helping your children build resilience and a growth mindset. Instead of seeing errors and failures as reflections of their intelligence or skill, allow them to see them as chances for learning and development. Give them encouragement and support for their efforts and advancements, and teach them to rise to challenges and endure in the face of difficulties. Offer a kind and encouraging atmosphere that acknowledges their accomplishments and motivates them to take chances and investigate novel prospects for education and development.

How can we respond to circumstances in which our kids are under pressure to perform well academically? How can we help them manage their stress and stay well?

Managing circumstances in which your kids are under pressure or stress related to their schoolwork entails offering them emotional support, assisting them in creating practical coping mechanisms, and encouraging a good balance between their schoolwork and personal time. Promote candid dialogue and attentive hearing, and accept their emotions and experiences without passing judgment. Assist them in identifying stressors and creating time and task management plans that include realistic goalsetting, task prioritization, and regular breaks. Give them the chance to partake in enjoyable and calming activities, such as hobbies, physical activity, or socializing with loved ones. Remind them that their well-being comes before academic success while praising and supporting their efforts and advancement.

In order for our kids to thrive in school and life, how can we support their development of critical thinking and problem-solving abilities?

Encouraging your kids to investigate and examine information, pose questions, and think critically and independently can help them develop their critical thinking and problem-solving abilities. As they hone their analytical and reasoning skills, mentor and assist them by asking questions and seeking solutions through investigation, testing, and discovery. Instruct students in the critical evaluation of information sources, how to separate opinion from reality, and assist them in creating efficient problem-solving techniques, including planning, brainstorming, and solution evaluation. Provide them credit and encouragement for their efforts and advancements, and offer them chances to use critical thinking in authentic settings and circumstances.

How can we help our kids develop a love of learning and curiosity, and why is it vital for their development both academically and personally?

Encouraging your children's natural interests and passions, offering opportunities for investigation and discovery, and creating a supportive and exciting learning environment are all essential ways to help them develop a love of learning and curiosity. Provide a range of learning opportunities and materials that suit their unique interests and learning preferences. Let them explore subjects and pursuits that pique their curiosity and keep them interested. Give them credit and encouragement for their interest and zeal as well as for their autonomous questioning, searching for solutions, and exploration of novel ideas and concepts. Fostering a passion for education not only helps students succeed academically but also encourages a lifelong love of learning and development.

How can we encourage our kids to explore and follow their passions and interests while also supporting their academic and career goals?

Helping your kids discover and follow their interests and passions entails offering them resources, support, and encouragement in order to help them achieve their academic and professional goals. Please encourage them to participate in a range of recreational and intellectual pursuits and provide them with chances to experience many professions and sectors firsthand. As students negotiate their academic and career pathways, assistance and encouragement should be given. Students should also be assisted in setting realistic goals and creating a plan of action. Provide direction and mentorship and put them in touch with opportunities and resources that suit their objectives and areas of interest. You can help them realize their potential and enthusiastically and confidently follow their dreams by supporting their interests and goals.

How can we help our kids build resilience and a growth mindset, and why are these traits crucial for their academic and personal progress?

Raising resilient children with a growth mindset entails encouraging a positive outlook on learning and development and offering assistance and support when they face obstacles and failures. Instead of seeing mistakes and failures as reflections of their intelligence or skill, help children to see them as chances for learning and development. Give them encouragement and support for their efforts and advancements, and teach them to rise to challenges and endure in the face of difficulties. You can give your kids the self-assurance and tenacity they need to excel in school and life by encouraging a growth mindset and resilience in them.

In order for our kids to thrive in school and beyond, how can we support them in creating productive study habits and academic skills?

Establishing a good and encouraging learning environment at home, as well as giving your kids discipline, direction, and support, are essential to helping them develop productive study habits and academic skills. Assist them in creating a regular study plan and routine, and offer a peaceful, cosy area where they can concentrate. Instruct them on inefficient study methods, including taking notes, planning, and managing their time, and provide support and direction as they grow in these abilities. Give them access to tools and resources for learning that are tailored to their unique interests and learning styles, and express gratitude.

Chapter Five

Relationship between internal and external family

What should we do when our opinions diverge on crucial parenting choices like healthcare, education, or discipline?

While disagreements over crucial parenting choices are common, they can be resolved by polite dialogue and mutual compromise. Begin by talking about each other's worries and points of view, then look for areas of agreement or different approaches that respect each partner's perspective. If the problem is too big for you to handle alone, think about getting advice from a family therapist, parenting coach, or any other reliable third party.

In cases where one partner's availability is restricted by their job or other obligations, how can we make sure that both are fully committed to and involved in parenting responsibilities?

Being flexible, willing to share the load, and engaging in proactive communication are necessary to guarantee equal participation in parenting responsibilities. Discuss each partner's preferences, strengths, and availability openly when it comes to parenting duties, and work together to divide up the work in a way that feels just and equal. Be prepared to change course when necessary to take into account new information and assist one another in striking a balance that benefits both parties.

How do we resolve disputes or conflicts about parenting choices or boundaries with inlaws or extended family members?

Assertive communication, setting boundaries, and maintaining a united front as a couple is necessary for handling conflicts or disagreements with inlaws or extended family. As a team, tackle the problem and firmly but respectfully voice your preferences or concerns. To safeguard your family's welfare and autonomy, establish clear expectations and boundaries with family members regarding their participation in parenting decisions or interactions with your children. Be ready to enforce these boundaries when needed.

How can we establish clear expectations and boundaries for our kids while simultaneously creating a happy and caring environment for them?

In addition to giving love, support, and direction, it is essential to establish clear expectations and boundaries in order to create a positive and supportive environment for kids. Openly discuss your beliefs, guidelines, and expectations with your kids. Also, set an example of polite conduct and communication by acting accordingly around them. Offer praise and encouragement for good behaviour and accomplishments, and be consistent in enforcing boundaries and consequences. You can foster a healthy, nurturing, and supportive environment in which your children can grow into resilient, self-assured adults.

How can we make sure that each partner feels equally essential and involved in raising their children?

Making decisions, providing care, and spending quality time with your kids all require active participation in order to ensure equal involvement and value in the parenting process. Talk honestly about your desire to participate and pay attention to one another's viewpoints. Look for ways to delegate tasks to each other and spend quality time as a family with your kids.

What should we do if we can't agree on rules or discipline techniques for our kids?

Try to understand each other's worries and points of view if you can't agree on rules or discipline techniques for your kids. By concentrating on your shared values and expectations for your kids' behaviour, you can find common ground. Think about trying out various strategies and being willing to make concessions. If necessary, get advice from parenting resources or expert assistance to come up with solutions that satisfy both parties.

How do we handle differences in cultural or marital expectations when it comes to parenting our children?

Handling variations in cultural or familial expectations includes acknowledging and respecting each other's backgrounds and opinions. Take the time to understand the cultural and family influences shaping each partner's parenting approach. Find common ground by concentrating on shared values and goals for your children's upbringing. Be open to learning from one other's cultural perspectives and be willing to change your parenting tactics accordingly.

What role does self-care play in effective parenting, and how can we ensure that both partners have opportunities for self-care while raising children?

Self-care is vital for sustaining physical, emotional, and mental well-being when parenting. Prioritize self-care activities that refresh and rejuvenate you, such as exercise, hobbies, or spending time with friends. Support each other in finding time for self-care by splitting parental tasks and offering to take breaks when required. Remember that taking care of yourself allows you to be a better parent and spouse to your family.

How can we assist our children to develop good communication skills and emotional intelligence within the family?

Encouraging healthy communication skills and emotional intelligence in children entails modelling positive communication and emotional expression as parents. Create a safe and supportive environment where children feel comfortable sharing their views and feelings. Practice active listening and empathy while interacting with your children, and teach them problem-solving skills and conflict-resolution tactics. Encourage open communication about emotions and acknowledge your children's experiences to help them create a strong foundation for successful relationships in the future.

What are some excellent ways for co-parenting with extended family members, like grandparents or siblings?

Coparenting with extended family members entails creating boundaries, conveying expectations, and finding common ground. Start by sharing your parenting ideals and preferences with your extended family members, and be clear about your boundaries and expectations when it comes to their engagement in your children's lives. Encourage open communication and flexibility, and be willing to compromise when necessary to maintain peace and respect within the family.

How do we handle arguments or disagreements with our children's teachers, caregivers, or other authority figures?
Handling confrontations with authority figures involves diplomacy, persuasion, and a focus on your children's best interests. Approach differences calmly and respectfully, and constructively share your concerns or viewpoints. Seek common ground and ideas that promote your children's well-being and academic achievement. Remember to model polite dispute resolution for your children and teach them how to advocate for themselves positively and assertively.

How can we develop a healthy relationship with technology and screen time within our family while simultaneously setting appropriate limitations and boundaries?
Promoting a healthy relationship with technology entails having clear expectations, modelling responsible use, and spending meaningful time together as a family. Establish screen time limits and boundaries that correspond with your family values

and priorities, and encourage alternative activities such as outdoor play, creative hobbies, and family dinners. Use technology as a tool for learning and communication rather than as a primary source of amusement, and prioritize creating strong connections and bonds with your children offline.

How can we establish reasonable restrictions and boundaries while yet encouraging a positive relationship between our family and technology and screen time?

Prioritizing quality time spent as a family, establishing clear expectations, and modelling responsible use are all critical in fostering a positive relationship with technology. Set screen time limitations and guidelines that suit your family's priorities and values. Promote outdoor play, creative hobbies, and family dinners as substitutes for screen time. Make it a priority to develop close relationships and ties with your children offline and use technology as a tool for learning and communication rather than as your primary source of pleasure.

How can we resolve disputes or problems with our kids' instructors, daycare providers, or other authority figures?

Resolving disputes with superiors calls for advocacy, diplomacy, and keeping your kids' best interests in mind. Resolve conflicts amicably and politely, and helpfully express your opinions or concerns. Look for areas of agreement and solutions that will improve your kids' academic performance and general well-being. Don't forget to set an example of polite dispute resolution for your kids and educate them on how to confidently and assertively stand up for themselves.

About the Author

ADEGBOYE S. ADURA GBEMI is a manager, business administrator, entrepreneur, and motivational speaker in Africa. ADEGBOYE has his BA from Yale University, IPMA from Adonai University, and a Master's in Business Administration (MBA) from the University of Salford, Manchester.

He was born in South Africa but is presently based in Nigeria as a motivational speaker and marriage counsellor in institutions, sectors, and seminars with young and upcoming managers all over Africa.

Acknowledgements

I want to express my sincere gratitude to everyone who helped with the "FAQ on Communication in Marriage." Throughout this journey, their encouragement, insight, and support have been priceless.

I want to start by acknowledging the fact that, without God, this guide wouldn't have been possibly achieved.

And also, to my spouse, who has always been motivating and supportive in making this task successful, I will always love and appreciate you.

I have many couples to appreciate who have shared their experiences, challenges, and victories with me over the years. Your openness, weakness, and tenacity have enhanced the book's pages and provided priceless insights into the difficulties of marriage communication.

My sincere gratitude goes out to my family and friends for their continuous support and encouragement during this journey. Your wise advice, tolerance, and words of support have helped me get through the complicated process of writing and releasing this book.

I sincerely thank the specialists and experts who have so kindly offered their knowledge and skills in marriage and communication. Your advice and thoughts have improved this book's quality and depth, and I really appreciate your contributions.

Finally, I would like to express my profound gratitude to all of the readers of this work. As you journey through the process of communication in your marriage, I hope that the knowledge, direction, and encouragement provided within these pages will be a source of inspiration and empowerment for you.

I sincerely appreciate your help.

www.ingramcontent.com/pod-product-compliance
Lightning Source LLC
Chambersburg PA
CBHW051243120626
46547CB00014B/1768